HOW THEY LIVED
IN
BIBLE TIMES

Graham Jones
Illustrated by
Richard and Christine Deverell

Regal Books

A Division of Gospel Light
Ventura, California, U.S.A.

MANHATTAN-ELWOOD
PUBLIC LIBRARY DISTRICT

Regal Books
A Division of Gospel Light
Ventura, California 93006
Printed in Great Britain

Library of Congress Cataloging-in-Publication Data
Jones, Graham, 1952-
     How they lived in Bible times / Graham Jones ; illustrated by Richard and Christine Deverell. — North American ed.
        p. cm.
     Includes index.
     Summary: Text and pictures portray life in the Middle East during the period spanned by the Bible.
     ISBN 0-8307-1511-8
     1. Jews—Social life and customs—To 70 A.D.—Juvenile literature. 2. Palestine—Social life and customs—To 70 A.D.—Juvenile literature. 3. Bible. O.T.—Antiquities—Juvenile literature. [1. Jews—Social life and customs—To 70 A.D. 2. Palestine—Social life and customs—To 70 A.D. 3. Bible. O.T.—Antiquities.]
I. Deverell, Richard, ill. II. Deverell, Christine, ill. III. Title.
DS112.J68 1992
933—dc20
                                                                                                              91-30420
                                                                                                                     CIP
                                                                                                                     AC

1 2 3 4 5 6 7 8 9 10   99 98 97 96 95 94 93 92 91

Contents

Today you probably started the day by getting dressed and having breakfast. You may have gone to school. How did you get there? By bicycle, bus, car or some other way? In your spare time you might have watched television or played a ball game. Perhaps later on you will read a story from the Bible and on Sunday you may go to church.

Have you ever thought what life was like for people in the Bible? Did they do the same things as you? What about the clothes they wore or the food they ate? How did they travel? What was school like? What did they do in their spare time and how did they learn about God?

Read on. You may find some answers.

God's rescue

The place is Jerusalem. The time – about 1100 years before the birth of Jesus. In a house near the city wall, the Hillel family has gathered for the Passover feast.

Passover is the most special day in the year. Tonight, every family in the land remembers an amazing rescue that happened about two hundred years before.

The Israelites had been slaves in Egypt for many years. Pharaoh, the king, treated them cruelly and refused to let them go free. There seemed to be no escape – until God stepped in.

The Israelites were slaves in Egypt. God sent Moses to talk to Pharaoh.

Moses told the Israelites that God had decided to punish the Egyptians.

Father Hillel tells the story

There is a special job at Passover for Jephthah. As the youngest in the family, he must ask his father to explain the meaning of the feast. So father fills his cup with wine and tells the story of how God rescued his people from Pharaoh, king of Egypt.

A time to return home

Israelites living outside Canaan try to get home for the Passover if they possibly can. Uncle Shaphan has just arrived from Syria. He lives near Damascus, where he makes a living trading camels.

A special meal

The night the Israelites left Egypt, they had to be ready to go at a moment's notice. So the last meal in Egypt had to be a quick one – roast lamb with bitter herbs and bread without yeast, which doesn't take as long to bake as ordinary bread. Each year, at Passover, every Israelite family eats the same meal again in memory.

But your children will [es]cape if each family kills a [la]mb and smears it's blood on the door

When are we going?

Soon, we must eat quickly

My son is dead! Take your people and get out of Egypt tonight!

[The] Israelites did as Moses said, then [wai]ted in their homes, eating their last [me]al in Egypt, ready for the order to move.

That night, the first son in every Egyptian family died. But God's angel passed over the houses of the Israelites. Their children were spared.

The Israelites were free at last.

The sign on the door

Father has sprinkled lamb's blood on the doorposts, just as his ancestors did on the first Passover night in Egypt.

Pots, pans, knives and cups must all be thoroughly cleaned before the Passover begins. Mother Hillel has spent the last day and a half sweeping and dusting the house from top to bottom.

Ready to go

On the first Passover night, the Israelites ate their meal ready and dressed for the long journey that was about to begin. Tonight the Hillels are wearing their outdoor clothes to remind themselves of that night.

After the meal, the family will sing hymns, praising God for rescuing the Israelites from Egypt.

The Hillel house has two levels inside. One is for people, the other for the family's animals.

Other festivals

Jephthah loves festivals. Nearly every month there's a celebration of some kind when the Hillels and all their neighbours get together to enjoy themselves and to thank God for looking after them. There's singing, and dancing and good things to eat, sometimes for days at a time.

The Feast of Weeks comes every year at the beginning of the harvest. Jephthah's father brings gifts to the priest – wheat, bread, an animal and some wine. When the animal has been killed, the priest burns part of it on the altar and gives back the rest so that all the family can have a picnic.

Grandad, why are we all sleeping outside?

When our ancestors left Egypt they didn't have nice houses... they had to live in tents. When we sleep outside, we remember what it must have been like.

The Feast of Booths comes in the autumn and lasts for a whole week. The Hillels and their friends bring more gifts to God and camp out at nights in shelters made of branches. They all have a good time to celebrate the end of the harvest.

Cooking the evening meal

About four hundred years have passed since the Passover feast on page 6. Hezekiah is now king of Israel. Hannah is a ten year old girl who lives in Jerusalem with her mother and father, her brothers and sisters, Aunt Hephzibah, Uncle Nabal and loads of cousins. Her house looks onto a courtyard which is shared by all the neighbours. It's nearly sunset – time to start cooking the evening meal.

Making butter

This bag contains goats' milk. As the women punch it from side to side, the milk turns to butter.

'Come back with that cheese!'

To make cheese, Hannah's mother mixes goat's milk with salt until it thickens, then lets it harden in the sun. Hannah loves it. So does the dog!

Some popular delicacies

- Camel's milk. (It's very rich, so it has to be diluted with water.)
- Locusts, often roasted on a skewer. See middle of picture.
- Sheep's tails.
- Pomegranate juice, especially in hot weather.

'Ouch! My back!'

Grinding flour is hard work. Aunt Hephzibah wishes they'd invent an easier way!

Olives

An olive tree. Some olives are eaten pickled; most are crushed to extract olive oil for cooking or for lighting.

It's all right for the men!

It's no good asking Uncle Nabal to help. Preparing food is strictly women's work.

Cookery for beginners

Lesson 1

Making bread

Water

Fetching water is back-breaking work. Most towns are built on hills, and the nearest spring is usually at the foot of the hill. So you carry your empty jar downhill and your full jar uphill! In Jerusalem it's slightly easier. A tunnel has been dug under the city wall to the spring nearby. To fetch water this evening, Hannah's sister, Deborah, has climbed down a flight of steps, walked along the tunnel and lowered a bucket on the end of a rope to fill her jar.

All-purpose cooker

Hannah's mother's oven is an earthenware jar sunk into the ground. Inside there's a fire. When the fire has died down, she sticks pancakes of dough against the inside walls to make bread. She can also put a pot on the top to make stews or heat water.

Vegetables for sale

Old Eli grows cucumbers, melons, leeks, onions, garlic, lentils and beans in a small garden outside Jerusalem. He sometimes sells figs and almonds as well.

Some customers – like this one – can be very choosy.

Goat stew

Athaliah, one of the neighbours, is making a goat's meat stew. The Bible allows Jews to eat any animal that has cloven hooves and also eats grass. So mutton and goat's meat are permitted, but pork is not. (Pigs have cloven hooves, but they don't eat grass.)

Question: Would the Hillels ever eat chicken? Answer below.

grind your grain. Use
r a quern and muller or
stle and mortar.

Add salt and water to make a nice gooey dough. Then add a handful of yesterday's dough to help it to rise.

Knead the dough well in a bowl. Cover with a cloth and leave for one hour.

Flatten the dough into thin pancakes, then bake in your mother's oven until crisp and golden.

No, the Jews didn't keep chickens until hundreds of years later. So no eggs for breakfast.

Herod's feast

It's now about thirty years since Jesus was born. Palestine has been conquered by the Romans who govern the Jews harshly.

Herod is in charge of Galilee in the northern part of Palestine. Although he's a Jew, he supports the Romans and the Romans keep him in power.

He lives in a fine, Roman-style palace in Tiberias on the shores of Lake Galilee. Roman soldiers guard him. He dresses like a Roman, talks like a Roman, eats like a Roman. His fellow Jews hate him.

Every so often, Herod holds a feast. The scene might have looked like this.

Show off!

Sextus is a government official and extremely wealthy. Before coming tonight he has taken a long bath and dressed up in sumptuous robes. If he really wants to show off, he'll send his servant home for another change of clothes before the meal is over.

Gift wrapping

Sometimes the guests would bring their own towels. If the host was feeling generous, he'd give out presents and the towels would be useful for carrying them home.

Dining couches

Herod's guests lie propped on their elbows on three sides of the dining table. The fourth side of the table is left clear so the servants can bring on the food.

M

Shellfish soup

Salt fish with olives

Pigs' livers

Flamingoes' tongues

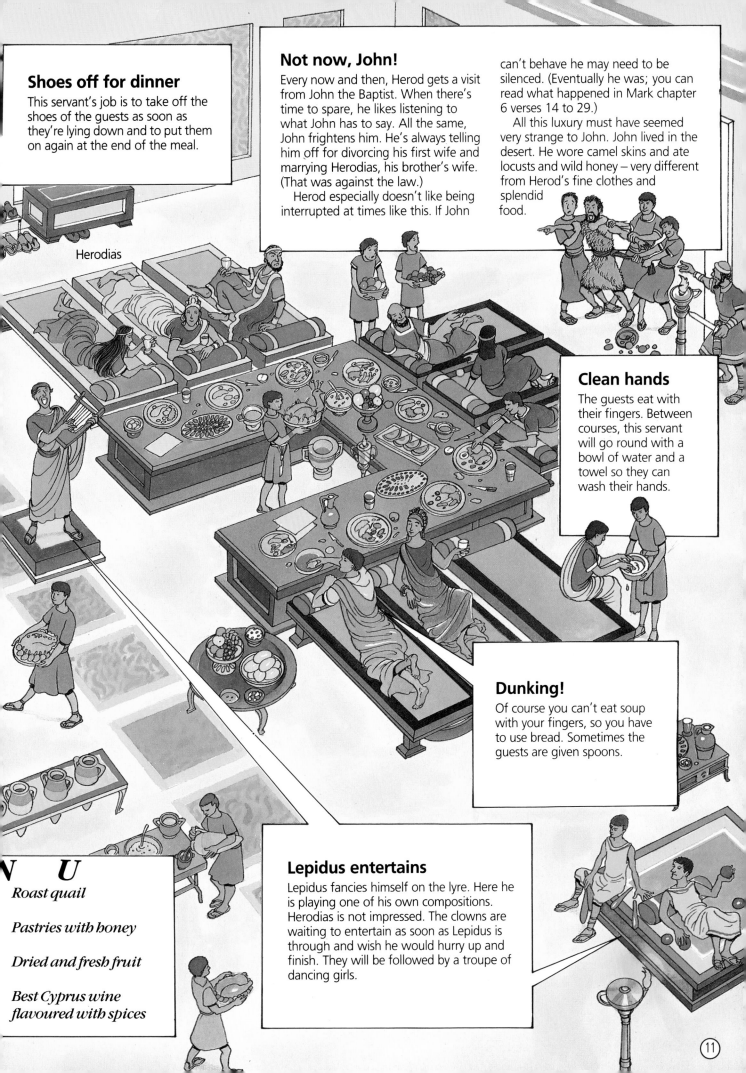

Shoes off for dinner

This servant's job is to take off the shoes of the guests as soon as they're lying down and to put them on again at the end of the meal.

Herodias

Not now, John!

Every now and then, Herod gets a visit from John the Baptist. When there's time to spare, he likes listening to what John has to say. All the same, John frightens him. He's always telling him off for divorcing his first wife and marrying Herodias, his brother's wife. (That was against the law.)

Herod especially doesn't like being interrupted at times like this. If John can't behave he may need to be silenced. (Eventually he was; you can read what happened in Mark chapter 6 verses 14 to 29.)

All this luxury must have seemed very strange to John. John lived in the desert. He wore camel skins and ate locusts and wild honey – very different from Herod's fine clothes and splendid food.

Clean hands

The guests eat with their fingers. Between courses, this servant will go round with a bowl of water and a towel so they can wash their hands.

Dunking!

Of course you can't eat soup with your fingers, so you have to use bread. Sometimes the guests are given spoons.

N U

Roast quail

Pastries with honey

Dried and fresh fruit

Best Cyprus wine flavoured with spices

Lepidus entertains

Lepidus fancies himself on the lyre. Here he is playing one of his own compositions. Herodias is not impressed. The clowns are waiting to entertain as soon as Lepidus is through and wish he would hurry up and finish. They will be followed by a troupe of dancing girls.

2000 years of fashion – from Abraham to Paul

About 1900 years before Jesus was born, an artist in Egypt painted a picture very like this on the wall of his master's tomb. It shows a desert chieftain from Canaan coming to Egypt with a group of tinkers or metalworkers. Who this chieftain is, we do not know. But

Abraham and his family would have looked very similar as they travelled from Canaan to Egypt. (To read the story, look at Genesis chapter 12.)

About 1200 years later, in a village near Jerusalem, Nathan and Abigail are getting married. Everyone has put on their best clothes. Nathan wears a white tunic and cloak, and his friends have put a

garland round his neck. The little boy at his side is Caleb, his nephew. He's acting as page boy and is dressed just like the bridegroom.

In the time of Nathan and Abigail's grandchildren, disaster struck the land of Judah. Nebuchadnezzar, king of Babylon, swept down from the north and conquered Jerusalem. His troops broke down the walls, burnt the city and took the people away to Babylon.

One of the captives was a young man named Daniel. On Nebuchadnezzar's orders, he has come to the palace to be trained as a servant. He still wears his plain Jewish clothes, in contrast to the splendid robes of the courtiers.

We have moved forward another 600 years. The Greeks and Romans have invaded the lands around the Mediterranean. Most people wear Greek-style clothes, including the apostle, Paul, and Timothy.

You can see them in the picture in long, close-fitting tunics, speaking to the crowd.
Notice the different sorts of shoes – the elaborate Greek sandals; the

The travellers are wearing embroidered tunics. The men have sandals, but some of the women are wearing boots. Notice what's missing: there are no hats. At the time this picture was painted, men wore hats only on special occasions.

Spot these objects: a lyre; bows and arrows; javelins; sticks for throwing; a skin water bottle; a scroll; goatskin bellows for making a good fire (very important for metalworkers).

Abigail has an embroidered wedding dress, with lots of jewellery round her neck. Her nose-ring is a wedding gift from Nathan. Under her veil she wears a string of coins across her forehead. These are her

dowry, a present from Nathan's family, and she'll treasure them all her life.

Nebuchadnezzar is very proud of his long, square beard. He spends hours every week having it curled into ringlets. His courtiers have copied the fashion. Earrings, necklaces, bracelets and arm bands are also popular.

Notice the visitors from Assyria. You can tell they're Assyrians because they wind their robes diagonally round their bodies. The Babylonians, on the other hand, let their robes hang straight.

fur-lined boots of the Roman soldier; the plain sandals of the poor farmer; the red leather boots worn by the man in the turban. There's even a man carrying his shoes to make them last longer!

Hairstyles have changed since the previous picture. The Romans have discovered how to make steel razors, so hair can be worn much shorter. Roman men and women often dye their hair or wear wigs.

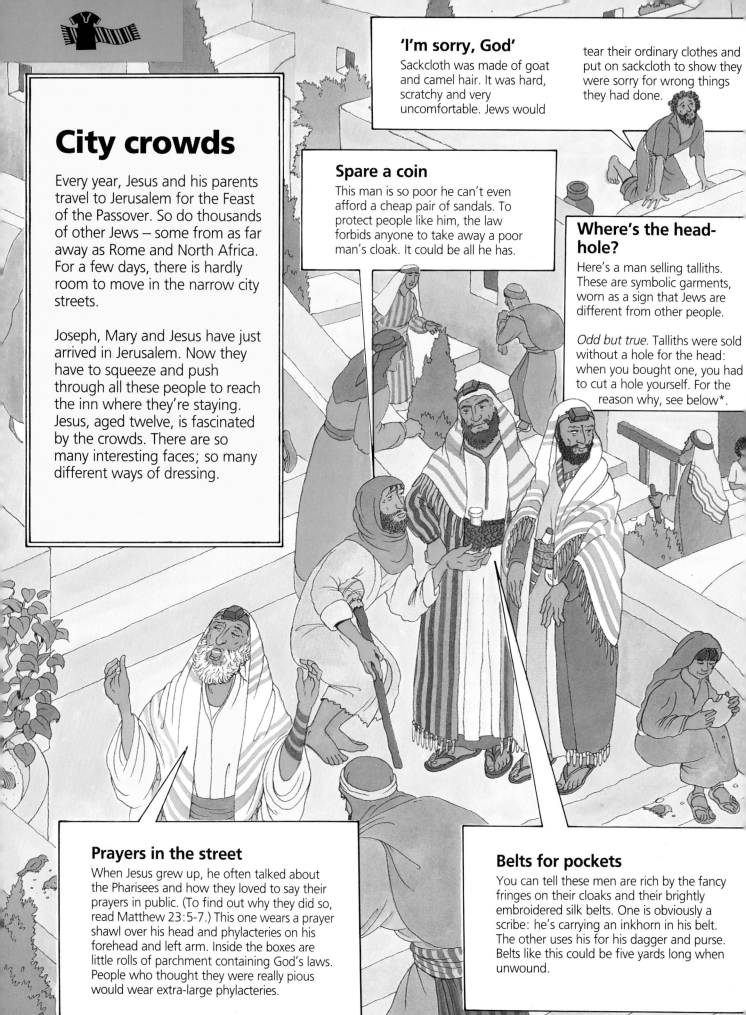

City crowds

Every year, Jesus and his parents travel to Jerusalem for the Feast of the Passover. So do thousands of other Jews – some from as far away as Rome and North Africa. For a few days, there is hardly room to move in the narrow city streets.

Joseph, Mary and Jesus have just arrived in Jerusalem. Now they have to squeeze and push through all these people to reach the inn where they're staying. Jesus, aged twelve, is fascinated by the crowds. There are so many interesting faces; so many different ways of dressing.

'I'm sorry, God'

Sackcloth was made of goat and camel hair. It was hard, scratchy and very uncomfortable. Jews would tear their ordinary clothes and put on sackcloth to show they were sorry for wrong things they had done.

Spare a coin

This man is so poor he can't even afford a cheap pair of sandals. To protect people like him, the law forbids anyone to take away a poor man's cloak. It could be all he has.

Where's the head-hole?

Here's a man selling talliths. These are symbolic garments, worn as a sign that Jews are different from other people.

Odd but true. Talliths were sold without a hole for the head: when you bought one, you had to cut a hole yourself. For the reason why, see below*.

Prayers in the street

When Jesus grew up, he often talked about the Pharisees and how they loved to say their prayers in public. (To find out why they did so, read Matthew 23:5-7.) This one wears a prayer shawl over his head and phylacteries on his forehead and left arm. Inside the boxes are little rolls of parchment containing God's laws. People who thought they were really pious would wear extra-large phylacteries.

Belts for pockets

You can tell these men are rich by the fancy fringes on their cloaks and their brightly embroidered silk belts. One is obviously a scribe: he's carrying an inkhorn in his belt. The other uses his for his dagger and purse. Belts like this could be five yards long when unwound.

*So you could be sure you were buying a new one.

Getting dressed

When Jesus got dressed this morning, he started with a knee-length tunic made of linen.

Then he put his belt on.

Then a woollen cloak.

He put sandals on his feet ...

... and on his head, a square of cloth folded into a triangle and held in place with a circle of cord.

Foreigner

This man has arrived from Persia. You can tell because he is wearing trousers and a felt hat.

Dressed for hard work

There is more than one way of wearing a tunic. These men have tucked the bottom of their tunics through their belts to leave their legs free for work.

The height of fashion.

The Pharisees won't like this! Here is a Jew wearing a toga. It was thought fashionable in some circles to abandon Jewish clothes and copy the styles of the Romans or Greeks.

The widow

Women dress very like the men, except that their clothes have more decoration. The main difference is the headgear. This woman wears a cap and a veil. The black veil shows she's a widow.

A palace for a queen

Solomon, king of Israel, has recently married the daughter of Pharaoh, king of Egypt. He wants nothing but the best for his new wife, and has decided she should have her very own palace. The building work is now under way.

In a few minutes from now, Solomon will take his wife to show her how the work is progressing. While he waits for her to get ready, he studies the plans for the new building with his architect.

The captain of the guard

Perfume dispensers

These are lumps of perfume that slowly melt into the hair and drip down over the body. (Feathers in your perfume cone certainly don't help!)

Egyptian gold

The Egyptians had a passion for gold and wore as much of it as they could. In the time of Solomon, Egyptian craftsmen were the best in the world at making gold jewellery.

When the Israelites left Egypt (see page 7), they took lots of Egyptian jewellery with them!

Keep that mirror still!

Egyptian ladies put black paint on their eyelids and green paint below their eyes. They also painted the palms of their hands and the soles of their feet.

Putting on make-up was not easy. The only mirrors were of polished metal, which reflected very poorly. You had to hold them still to be able to see.

The vulture on the Princess's head-dress is a symbol of royalty.

Egyptian priest

(Solomon's queen has brought this priest with her from Egypt. You can tell he's a priest by his leopard skin.)

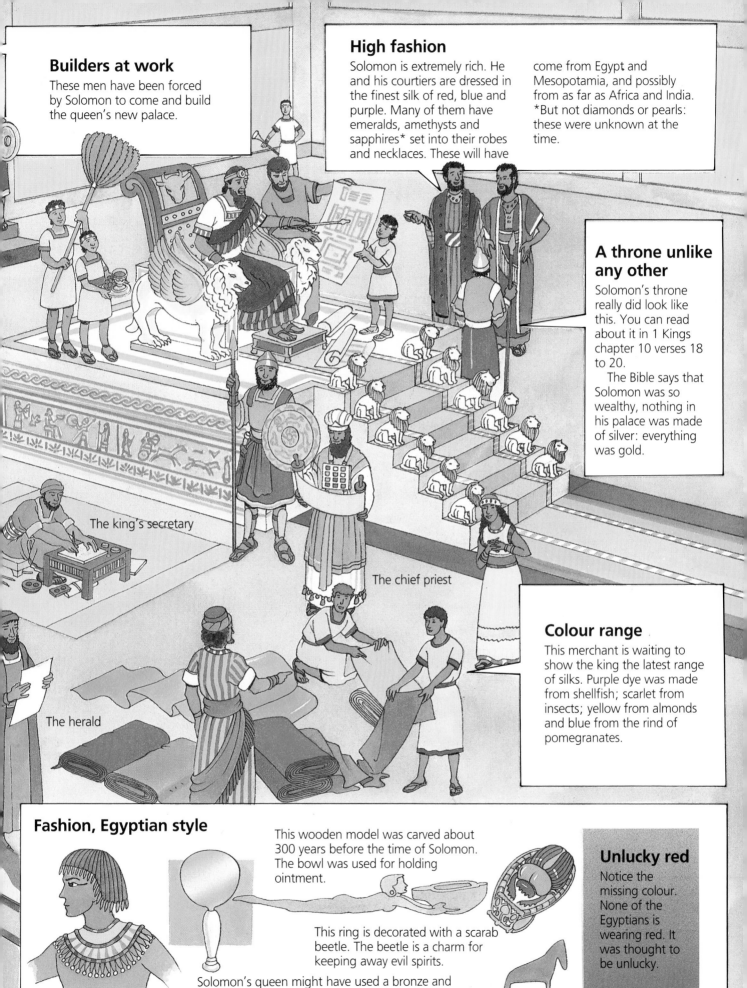

Builders at work

These men have been forced by Solomon to come and build the queen's new palace.

High fashion

Solomon is extremely rich. He and his courtiers are dressed in the finest silk of red, blue and purple. Many of them have emeralds, amethysts and sapphires* set into their robes and necklaces. These will have come from Egypt and Mesopotamia, and possibly from as far as Africa and India. *But not diamonds or pearls: these were unknown at the time.

A throne unlike any other

Solomon's throne really did look like this. You can read about it in 1 Kings chapter 10 verses 18 to 20.

The Bible says that Solomon was so wealthy, nothing in his palace was made of silver: everything was gold.

The king's secretary

The chief priest

The herald

Colour range

This merchant is waiting to show the king the latest range of silks. Purple dye was made from shellfish; scarlet from insects; yellow from almonds and blue from the rind of pomegranates.

Fashion, Egyptian style

This wooden model was carved about 300 years before the time of Solomon. The bowl was used for holding ointment.

This ring is decorated with a scarab beetle. The beetle is a charm for keeping away evil spirits.

Solomon's queen might have used a bronze and ivory mirror like this.

Rich Egyptian men used to wear collars made of gold or silver and decorated with jewels.

An Egyptian comb.

Unlucky red

Notice the missing colour. None of the Egyptians is wearing red. It was thought to be unlucky.

Isaac's camp

Isaac and Rebekah are nomads, travelling the desert and pitching their tents wherever they can find water. They have twin sons, Esau and Jacob, who are now about twelve years old. They also have a large number of animals and servants who travel with them.

When they stop, Isaac pitches his tent in the centre of the camp and the servants put theirs around the edges.

It's a tough life being a nomad. Wild animals, unfriendly neighbours and raiding Philistines can all make trouble – often at the same time.

Spies

Here are two Philistines spying on Isaac's camp. When it's dark, they'll call their friends and creep down and fill up the well with earth. Tomorrow, Isaac's servants will have to dig it all over again.

These mats are used for sleeping on.

This water bottle is made of a whole goatskin.

Just like modern tents, Isaac's home is held up by ropes, pinned to the ground with pegs.

The home

Isaac's tent is made of goats' hair, woven into strips which are then sewn together. It's divided into two halves, one for men and the other for women. The poles have hooks in them for hanging clothes, cooking pots and other useful things.

There isn't much in Isaac's tent, because all his belongings have to be carried on donkeys or camels when he moves. There's no furniture. Mats or carpets have to do as chairs. For a table, Rebekah simply lays an animal skin on the ground.

The trickster

Jacob is helping his mother to weave a new coat. He and his brother are very different. Esau likes hunting, exploring and fighting bears. Jacob would much rather stay at home and help around the tent.

In Genesis chapter 27, you can read of a mean trick that Jacob played on Esau.

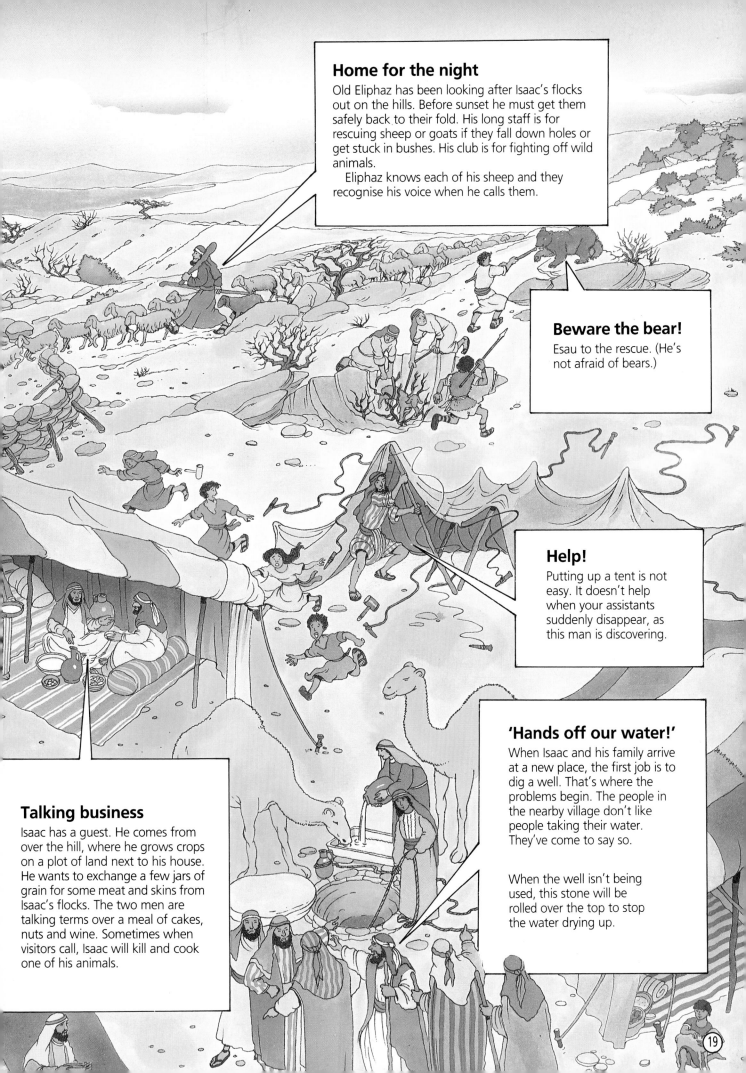

Home for the night

Old Eliphaz has been looking after Isaac's flocks out on the hills. Before sunset he must get them safely back to their fold. His long staff is for rescuing sheep or goats if they fall down holes or get stuck in bushes. His club is for fighting off wild animals.

Eliphaz knows each of his sheep and they recognise his voice when he calls them.

Beware the bear!

Esau to the rescue. (He's not afraid of bears.)

Help!

Putting up a tent is not easy. It doesn't help when your assistants suddenly disappear, as this man is discovering.

'Hands off our water!'

When Isaac and his family arrive at a new place, the first job is to dig a well. That's where the problems begin. The people in the nearby village don't like people taking their water. They've come to say so.

When the well isn't being used, this stone will be rolled over the top to stop the water drying up.

Talking business

Isaac has a guest. He comes from over the hill, where he grows crops on a plot of land next to his house. He wants to exchange a few jars of grain for some meat and skins from Isaac's flocks. The two men are talking terms over a meal of cakes, nuts and wine. Sometimes when visitors call, Isaac will kill and cook one of his animals.

Homes

Homes in the rock

Thousands of years ago, many people in Palestine lived in caves. These could be made quite comfortable. A strong door would keep out wild animals, and seats could be made by cutting ledges in the rock. There was no chimney of course, so the fire would be near the entrance to allow the smoke out.

Caves made a good place for robber gangs to hide. And not just robbers, either. When David was on the run from King Saul, he and his men hid in caves in the desert.

It's possible that the stable where Jesus was born was a cave rather like this one.

Goat-skin tents

Abraham, Isaac and Jacob all lived in tents. These were originally made of animal skins, though later on people started using goats' hair. This was woven into strips which were then sewn together. You can tell from the colours of the strips that most goats in Palestine were either black or brown.

Goats' hair is ideal for the job. It's waterproof, it keeps out the heat, and when it is washed it shrinks and becomes taut. The best goats' hair of all came from Cilicia near the city of Tarsus. (This area is now part of Turkey.) The people of Tarsus were famous for making good tents. Tarsus was Paul's home, and Paul was a tentmaker as well as a travelling preacher.

Houses made of mud

After the Jews had escaped from Egypt (see page 6), they travelled through the desert to Canaan. The journey took forty years. Along the way, living in tents, the people must have longed for the time when they could once again live in proper houses.

The houses in Canaan were made of mud bricks and shaped like beehives. They were probably very uncomfortable – dark, stuffy and full of insects. The whole family would live in one room along with their animals. When it rained, the roof would drip constantly.

Keeping burglars out was practically impossible. All a robber had to do was break a hole in one of the walls.

One-roomed homes

Once the Jews were settled in Canaan, they started to build houses of stone rather than mud. These were still not very solid. The mortar holding the stones together dissolved easily if it got wet. After a heavy downpour, whole villages could end up in ruins.

The roofs were made by laying beams across the tops of the walls, covering them with branches and finishing off with a layer of clay. After rain, the clay surface would have to be rolled smooth again with a small stone roller.

In this type of house, the whole family lived in one room. The upper level was for sleeping and eating, while the area below was used for sheltering the animals at night.

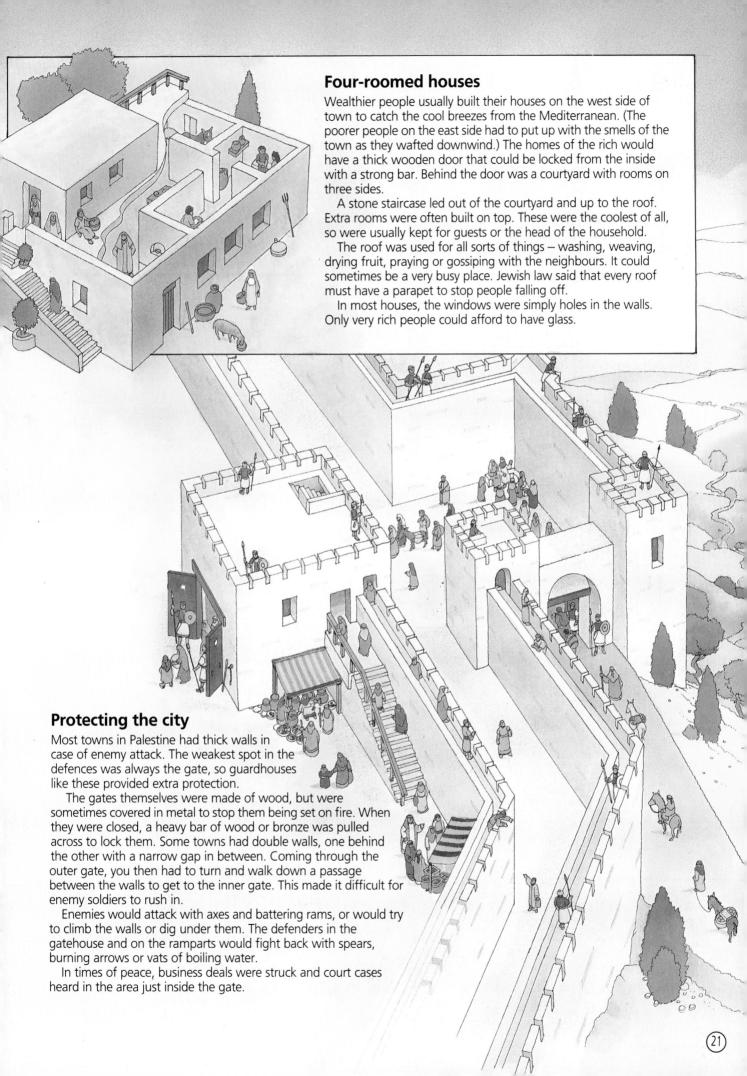

Four-roomed houses

Wealthier people usually built their houses on the west side of town to catch the cool breezes from the Mediterranean. (The poorer people on the east side had to put up with the smells of the town as they wafted downwind.) The homes of the rich would have a thick wooden door that could be locked from the inside with a strong bar. Behind the door was a courtyard with rooms on three sides.

A stone staircase led out of the courtyard and up to the roof. Extra rooms were often built on top. These were the coolest of all, so were usually kept for guests or the head of the household.

The roof was used for all sorts of things – washing, weaving, drying fruit, praying or gossiping with the neighbours. It could sometimes be a very busy place. Jewish law said that every roof must have a parapet to stop people falling off.

In most houses, the windows were simply holes in the walls. Only very rich people could afford to have glass.

Protecting the city

Most towns in Palestine had thick walls in case of enemy attack. The weakest spot in the defences was always the gate, so guardhouses like these provided extra protection.

The gates themselves were made of wood, but were sometimes covered in metal to stop them being set on fire. When they were closed, a heavy bar of wood or bronze was pulled across to lock them. Some towns had double walls, one behind the other with a narrow gap in between. Coming through the outer gate, you then had to turn and walk down a passage between the walls to get to the inner gate. This made it difficult for enemy soldiers to rush in.

Enemies would attack with axes and battering rams, or would try to climb the walls or dig under them. The defenders in the gatehouse and on the ramparts would fight back with spears, burning arrows or vats of boiling water.

In times of peace, business deals were struck and court cases heard in the area just inside the gate.

Country life

Jonathan lives in a village a few miles from the city of Samaria. It's just over 900 years before the birth of Jesus and Jeroboam is king of Israel. These are some of the things Jonathan might have done during the year.

Learning to plough

Jonathan gets a lesson from Zedekiah, the village ploughman. Og the ox – a stubborn, bad-tempered animal – is not being very helpful.

The blade of the plough is little more than a pointed stick. It needs a lot of concentration to keep the furrow straight.

Zedekiah has one of the new-style ploughs with an iron point. Previously, the points were made of stone or wood and quickly got broken.

Scaring the birds

Before the seed can be sown, the whole family must get to work to clear the field of stones. It's a back-breaking job and Jonathan hates it. It's much more fun scaring off the birds while his father scatters the seed.

When the sowing is finished, they'll bring back Og to plough the field again and cover the seed up.

The stones are heaped at the side of the field to mark the boundary. It's a serious crime to move the pile to try and make the field bigger.

Treading grapes

The wine harvest is fun for everybody. Jonathan loves squelching up and down in the wine press, getting smeared from head to toe in grape juice.

As the grapes are pulped, the juice flows down the channel to a nearby basin cut in the rock. When the pips and skin have sunk to the bottom, the juice is put into goatskins and left to ferment.

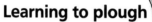

Beating olives

Two months after the grape harvest it's time to pick the olives. This is done by beating the trees with long poles. As soon as Jonathan gets out of the tree, the work will begin.

Trapping

Jonathan's elder brother, Tubal, is hoping to catch a partridge for supper. But making a trap is harder than he thinks. He isn't having much success.

Gathering sheaves

Six months later the wheat is harvested. Jonathan's father and brothers have new sickles – iron ones instead of the old flint ones. They're much faster. Jonathan's job is to collect the sheaves and he can hardly keep up.

Some of the wheat in the corners of the field won't be cut. It will be left for the poor people of the village to collect for themselves.

Threshing the wheat

After harvesting, the sheaves of wheat are scattered on the threshing floor and Og pulls the threshing sledge round and round. The sledge has stones fixed to its underside. These grind the sheaves and separate the grain from the stalks. The heavier the sledge, the better the job will be done.

Jonathan and his friends are trying to see how many children can ride on the sledge.

There's some consolation for Og. Jewish law says he must be allowed to stop and munch the wheat if he wants to.

At the olive press

Olive oil is used for cooking. It also provides fuel for lamps around the house. The olives used to be crushed by foot in the wine press. Now it's done differently. Jonathan's father has just built this modern-style press that grinds the fruit with a big stone.

In the carpenter's shop

There's always something to be made or mended – a door, a gate, a ladder, a chair. This time it's a new cart for Og.

Making bricks

Uncle Amos wants to build a new house. The first job is making the bricks and all the family helps. The bricks are made of mud and straw. They're shaped in a mould, then left in the sun to dry for a couple of days. After that they'll be stacked and left for another three weeks to get really hard.

Going shopping

When Jesus visited Jerusalem, he must often have stopped and watched people at work in their shops. These are some of the sights he might have seen.

The jeweller

To purify silver, the jeweller first melts it in a little bowl, then blows on it through a pipe to separate the impurities from the silver itself. His assistant is drilling holes in some beads before threading them onto a necklace.

The scribe

If you don't know how to write, this man will do your letters for you. He writes on papyrus with a reed pen and scrapes out mistakes with a small knife.

The potter

Everybody needs pots, so the potters in Jerusalem are kept very busy. This potter spins the wheel with his feet, leaving both hands free to shape the pot. When he has finished, the pot will be left to dry, decorated, then baked hard in the kiln.

Heads or tails?

Under Roman law, the Jews can have their own coins of bronze or copper, but are not allowed to make gold or silver coins. Only the Romans can do that. Some Roman coins have the head of the Emperor on them. Jewish coins always show plants or symbols. (To discover why they never showed people's heads, read Exodus chapter 20 verse 4.)

A Jewish shekel   A Greek tetradrachm   A Roman denarius   A Roman quadrans

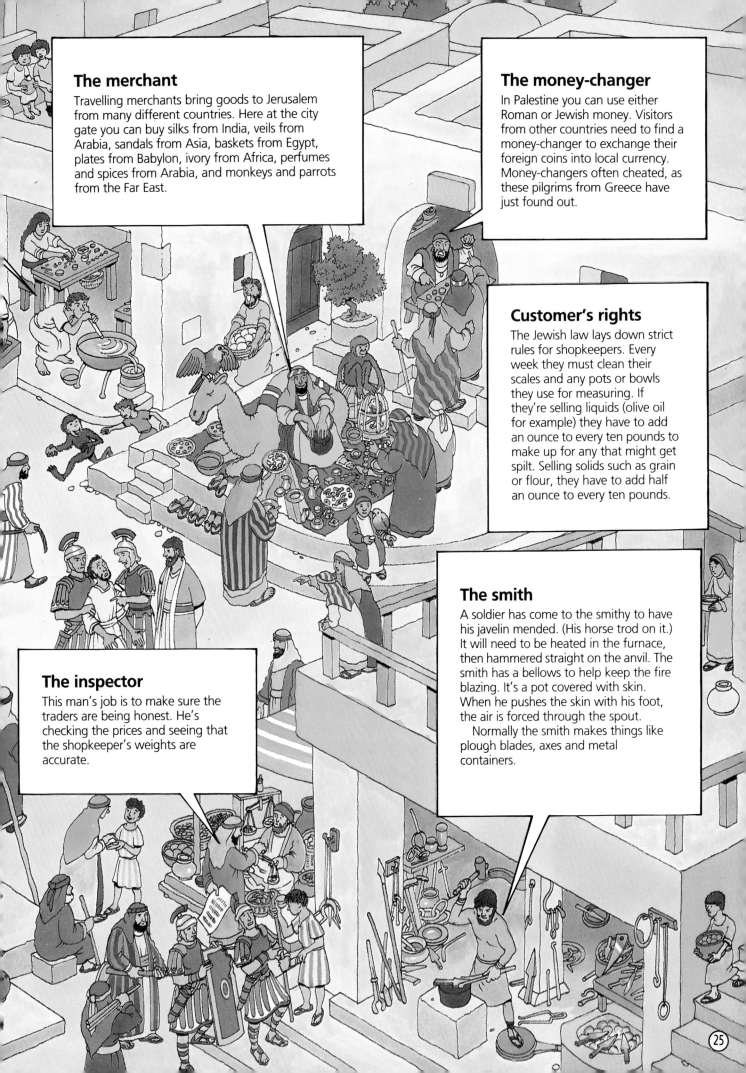

The merchant

Travelling merchants bring goods to Jerusalem from many different countries. Here at the city gate you can buy silks from India, veils from Arabia, sandals from Asia, baskets from Egypt, plates from Babylon, ivory from Africa, perfumes and spices from Arabia, and monkeys and parrots from the Far East.

The money-changer

In Palestine you can use either Roman or Jewish money. Visitors from other countries need to find a money-changer to exchange their foreign coins into local currency. Money-changers often cheated, as these pilgrims from Greece have just found out.

Customer's rights

The Jewish law lays down strict rules for shopkeepers. Every week they must clean their scales and any pots or bowls they use for measuring. If they're selling liquids (olive oil for example) they have to add an ounce to every ten pounds to make up for any that might get spilt. Selling solids such as grain or flour, they have to add half an ounce to every ten pounds.

The smith

A soldier has come to the smithy to have his javelin mended. (His horse trod on it.) It will need to be heated in the furnace, then hammered straight on the anvil. The smith has a bellows to help keep the fire blazing. It's a pot covered with skin. When he pushes the skin with his foot, the air is forced through the spout.

Normally the smith makes things like plough blades, axes and metal containers.

The inspector

This man's job is to make sure the traders are being honest. He's checking the prices and seeing that the shopkeeper's weights are accurate.

Moses at school

We've moved on about 600 years from the time of Abraham (page 12). His descendants, the Israelites, have settled in Egypt. There are now so many of them, the Egyptians are worried they'll take over the whole country. Pharaoh, the king, has put the Israelites to work as slaves. He has also ordered that all baby boys born to Israelite families should be drowned in the River Nile.

One Israelite boy has escaped. (You can read how in Exodus chapter 2 verses 1 to 10.) His name is Moses. Pharaoh's daughter has adopted him as her son, and he now lives in Pharaoh's palace.

Today Moses and the other royal children are having lessons. The class is copying a hymn to the sun-god, Re. Moses would much rather be outside playing.

Target practice

The Egyptians are very good archers. Their bows are made of wood and animal horn glued together. The arrows are reeds with bronze heads

These baboons have been specially trained to pick figs.

Writing materials

There's no blackboard in Moses' class. The teacher writes the words on a wooden board coated in wax. When he has finished, the board can be waxed again and reused. The pupils are scratching on bits of broken pottery that can be thrown away when the lesson is over. For very important work, they write on papyrus.

Toys

Much more fun than lessons ... models like these are popular toys. So are hoops and spinning tops.

How to make papyrus

Take several strips of papyrus reed and lay them side by side.

Lay some more strips horizontally across them.

Press them together and allow them to dry in the sun.

When the strips are dry, rub them smooth with a stone. The papyrus is now ready for writing on.

To make a scroll, glue several sheets of papyrus side by side.

Farming

There is hardly any rain in Egypt, so all the water for the fields has to come from the Nile. This farmer is using a 'shaduf'. On one end of the pole is a leather bucket; on the other end is a stone weight. He swings the pole down, scoops up water in the bucket and tips it into the ditches that carry the water to the crops.

Rehearsal in progress

Some of the ladies of the palace are practising a dance for Pharaoh's banquet tonight. The instruments are a harp, a lute and a set of double pipes.

Fishing

Another Egyptian skill — catching fish with spears.

Board game

This game is called 'senet'. The palace championship is in full swing. The players throw knuckle bones to decide the moves.

Ouch!

These are beehives. The old slave is teaching the young one how to get rid of the bees by smoking them out. When the bees have been removed, they'll be able to get at the honey.

Moses' pen set

When Moses writes on papyrus he uses a pen made of reed. His pen case has two or three reed pens and some cakes of ink. He writes by dipping the reed in water and moistening the ink.

Egyptian writing

Instead of using letters, the Egyptians write in pictures called hieroglyphs. This hieroglyph means 'Egypt'.

Every day is a learning day

This is the family of Simeon and Leah. They live in a house in Capernaum on the shores of Lake Galilee. Simeon is a fisherman and he and Leah have six children.

It's a proud day for Caleb. Last week he was thirteen, and his father brought him to the synagogue for a special ceremony called 'barmitzvah'. Here he became 'a son of the Law'. This shows he has now become an adult. He's allowed to wear a prayer shawl and phylactery. When he comes to the synagogue, he no longer has to sit with the women and children in the gallery, but can come downstairs with the men.

In the synagogue today there's a new preacher from Nazareth. He's called Jesus. Caleb and his father agree he's the best preacher they've ever heard.

A phylactery – a little leather box containing God's commandments on rolls of parchment. Jewish men would wear them on their arm and forehead.

Zebedee is ten. It's time for him to learn a trade, so Simeon is teaching him to throw a fishing net. One day he'll be expert at it.

School is for boys only, and they start when they're about six. Thomas is now eight. He goes to school at the synagogue and spends several hours a day learning the Bible by heart. There are not many school holidays!

Teachers in Palestine are highly respected. They have to be married, and they're not allowed to punish their pupils too much. If they do, they can lose their jobs.

Martha is Thomas' twin sister. When Thomas goes to school, she stays at home and learns how to cook and clean, or make and mend the family's clothes.

Here she's helping to spin thread from wool. First Martha rolls the wool into strands, then her mother runs it over her shoulder and twists it onto a pair of spindles to make the thread.

Like most girls in Palestine, Martha will probably be married by the time she's sixteen. Her husband will expect her to be well trained.

Esther is five and Samuel is only three, but already they know lots of stories from the Bible. Every day Leah tells them a new one. Today they're hearing how the walls of Jericho came tumbling down as their ancestors entered the Promised Land. (You can read the story for yourself in Joshua chapter 6.)

Some games never change. Martha is playing hop-scotch.

'Give thanks to the Lord!'

It's the beginning of October, about 600 years after the passover feast on page 6. The corn, the grapes and the olives have all been harvested. Now is the time to thank God for his goodness. Everybody stops work to praise God and celebrate 'the Feast of Booths'. The party goes on for eight whole days.

Praising God

The singers are singing a verse from a psalm: 'The land has produced its harvest; God, our God has blessed us.' (Psalm 67, verse 6)

Poor Bildad

Tomorrow is the last day of the feast. Bildad the bullock will be sacrificed, and the whole village will have a roast-beef dinner.

When I was in Babylon ...

Here's another cause for celebration. Uncle Daniel has moved back to the village from Babylon, where he's lived for many years. He seems to have some exciting stories to tell.

'Come back with that rope!'

The children are playing some very familiar games – leapfrog, blind man's buff, hide and seek and tug o' war (when Ben brings the rope back).

Outdoor living

For this one week in the year, the people build shelters or booths out in the open and sleep in them at night. That's why the festival is called 'the Feast of Booths'. Sleeping out of doors, people remember how their ancestors long ago had to live in tents in the desert.

Making music

A cane flute

The pipe was a favourite instrument with children.

A lyre decorated with silver and ivory.

A trumpet made of ram's horn.

Cymbals.

This harp provides the bass notes.

A lute.

Tambourines – very popular at feasts and in processions.

Good mover!

Uncle Amos is showing off! Last year he just missed getting the prize for best dancer. This year he's determined to win it.

Fact: Unlike modern times, the men and women always danced separately.

Just like the old days

What a party! Grandad has seen some great feasts in his time, but this one beats them all.

At the races

We're in Jerusalem just a few months before the birth of Jesus. The king, Herod the Great, has built a magnificent sports stadium and decorated the outside with gold, silver and precious stones. Today there is chariot racing, with a huge bag of gold for the winner.

As the charioteers prepare and the crowds gather, Simon comes by with his father. Simon wants to go in, but his father shakes his head. 'Chariots and fighting and things like that are all right for Romans, but not for decent Jews. Terrible things happen inside there. You don't want anything to do with them.'

Most Jews detest the dangerous and cruel sports of the Greeks and Romans. But they have to put up with them. Chariot racing and gladiatorial combat are regular events in Herod's Jerusalem.

Favourite pastimes of the Greeks and Romans

A chariot race is seven laps of the stadium – about six miles. Crashes are frequent and drivers are often killed, but the winners are awarded huge prizes.

The Greeks are very fond of athleti Jews disapprove because the contestants are often naked and athletics matches are dedicated to pagan gods.

Jewish pastimes

In this game, children dig a trench and see how many pebbles they can throw into it from a distance.

The Jews may not approve of Greek wrestling, but they enjoy their own type of wrestling match. You can read about one famous bout in Genesis chapter 32, verses 24 to 26.

Bullseye! Some Jewish boys can sling a stone with amazing accuracy.

e Romans love shows in which adiators fight to the death. Some ht with a net and trident, others th a sword and shield.

Theatre-going is a favourite Greek pastime. A few theatres exist in Palestine, and touring companies put on shows and plays. There are even a few Jewish actors, though devout Jews never attend.

e travelling storyteller is vays popular. He tells es of Jewish heroes and God's love for his ople.

Worshipping God

When the Israelites wanted to worship God or ask forgiveness for things they had done wrong, they would sometimes bring an animal to the temple to be sacrificed. It had to be one of their best animals. It was placed on the altar and killed by one of the priests.

Once a year, all the Israelites came to the temple for the Day of Atonement. On this very solemn occasion, all the people asked God to forgive the wrong they had done. The scene in the temple, in Old Testament times, might have looked like this.

The High Priest

On the Day of Atonement, the High Priest sacrifices a fine, strong goat to ask God's forgiveness for everything the people have done wrong.

The job of High Priest is passed from father to son. All High Priests are descended from Aaron, the brother of Moses.

But why do we need to have sacrifices?

Well, God is holy, and that means when we do something wrong, we ought to be punished. But he also loves us. He has said he will forgive us if we offer a sacrifice.

Amos the prophet

God is constantly sending prophets to remind the people that sacrifices on their own are not enough. To please God, they must do good in their everyday lives and fight against injustice. This is the prophet Amos, just in from the country to watch what's going on.

Followers of Jesus

When Jesus died, his followers at first thought it was a terrible mistake. Then they started to see that his death was really a sacrifice. It meant all their sins were forgiven – forever. No more sacrifices would ever be needed again.

To begin with, Jesus' followers worshipped God in the temple, just as they always had done. Later they began meeting in one another's houses. When they met, they would share a meal in memory of Jesus' death. This house is almost overflowing because so many people want to find out about Jesus.

Bread and wine

The meal of bread and wine reminds the disciples of Jesus' sacrifice. The bread stands for his body; the wine for his blood. (In today's communion service, Christians remember Jesus' death in the same way.)

Singing

Whenever they meet, the Christians sing praises to God for sending Jesus to be their friend.

He did. But now he's alive. He's our friend forever.

Why are we singing to Jesus? I thought he died.

Helping a brother

Being a Christian is not easy. Felix has just lost his job for refusing to worship the Roman Emperor. Other Christians have even been killed for believing in Jesus.

Sharing

All possessions are shared. Sextus has two coats, so he has given one to Jude who doesn't have one.

The scapegoat

This goat is called the scapegoat. The High Priest has just placed his hands on its head and asked God to let the goat take the blame instead of the people. It is now being chased away into the desert, carrying the people's sins with it. It will never be seen again.

Worshipping other gods

The Israelites worshipped one God. That made them very unusual, because the nations around them worshipped lots of different gods. There were gods of the sun and moon, gods of rain and thunder, gods of harvest, gods of love and gods of war. The Romans even had a god of the drains!

Each nation made up stories about its gods. Some were evil and some were kind. Mostly they behaved just like human beings – marrying, fighting, plotting and so on. The way to be prosperous and successful, people thought, was to please the gods by making sacrifices. This sometimes involved cruel practices such as offering children as human sacrifices.

The God of Israel constantly told his people not to worship other gods. Sometimes they obeyed him; sometimes they refused to listen.

Egyptian gods

The Egyptians treated their gods like kings. These priests have 'woken up' a statue of Osiris, god of the dead, by singing hymns. Now they are washing him. Soon they will dress him and give him food to see him through the day.

The Egyptians thought that when people died, they had really gone to another world. When they buried somebody, they also buried food, clothing and other belongings that might be needed in the next life.

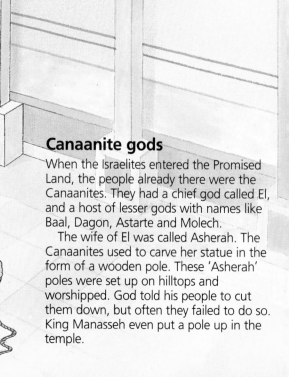

Canaanite gods

When the Israelites entered the Promised Land, the people already there were the Canaanites. They had a chief god called El, and a host of lesser gods with names like Baal, Dagon, Astarte and Molech.

The wife of El was called Asherah. The Canaanites used to carve her statue in the form of a wooden pole. These 'Asherah' poles were set up on hilltops and worshipped. God told his people to cut them down, but often they failed to do so. King Manasseh even put a pole up in the temple.

Babylonian gods

King Nebuchadnezzar of Babylon once erected a golden statue 28 metres high and ordered his people to worship it. (You can read the story in Daniel chapter 3 and see what happened to three brave Israelites who refused.)

The story in the Bible does not tell us whose statue it was. It might have been Adad, the god of storms; Sin the moon-god; Nergal, god of diseases; or Ishtar, the goddess of love. Or it might have been a statue of Nebuchadnezzar himself. Babylonian kings were often regarded as gods.

Roman gods

The Romans had some gods of their own, but also worshipped gods that belonged to other countries. For example, the Roman gods Jupiter, Mars and Venus were really Greek gods with different names. The Romans also worshipped the Egyptian goddess, Isis, and the Persian god, Mithras. Mithras was very important. His job was to protect the Roman army.

Each family would also have its gods. There would be a shrine in a corner of the home, and every day the father of the family would offer the gods food and wine.

Jacob goes to Egypt

We last saw Jacob on page 18. Then he was a boy. Now he's an old man with twelve sons and fifty-six grandchildren.
Today is possibly the greatest day of his life.
Many years ago his favourite son, Joseph, was lost. Jacob thought he'd been killed by wild animals. What really happened was that Joseph's brothers sold him to some merchants who took him to Egypt. In Egypt, Joseph became rich and powerful – the most important man after the king.
Old Jacob has just discovered that Joseph is still alive. His other sons have been to Egypt, met Joseph and brought back the news. Joseph wants all the family to move to Egypt to be with him. He has even sent some wagons to transport them.
It's going to be a long, slow journey. Egypt is two hundred miles away over rough and difficult country, but Jacob is determined to go. In a few minutes the wagons will start to roll.

Food for the journey

Corn, bread and other provisions provided by Joseph for the long journey. They will need plenty of supplies. The road to Egypt will later take the travellers across the scorching desert.

Bone shakers

Joseph has sent these wooden-wheeled wagons from Egypt. Where Jacob lives in Canaan, wagons are a strange sight. Because the country is so hilly and the roads are just tracks, most people get about by donkey or on foot.

'I thought we were travelling light!'

"Don't worry about your belongings," said Pharaoh, king of Egypt, as Joseph's brothers left to fetch their father from Canaan. "You'll find everything you need when you arrive."
Jacob isn't so sure. He'd rather be on the safe side and take *everything*. His eldest son, Reuben, thinks maybe they don't need quite so many cooking pots.

Time to set off

Journeys have to begin at dawn or even earlier, because very soon the day gets too hot for travelling.

Eighty for Egypt

It's a big crowd – about eighty people plus several hundred sheep and goats, a few dozen donkeys and a couple of camels.

Luxury travel

Camels are perfect for travelling in the desert. They can carry about half a ton and their slit nostrils and long eyelashes keep out blowing sand. Their humps are stores of fat that can keep them going for long periods without food. They can also go for days without water. All the same, camels were used only occasionally in Jacob's time. They didn't become really popular until hundreds of years later.

Souvenirs from Egypt

Joseph gave his brothers fine Egyptian clothing to take back to Canaan with them. Here they are in their pleated linen skirts and fancy belts with long tabs.

Woolly money

You can tell how wealthy somebody is by the number of sheep and goats he has. Jacob is not poor – and all his flocks and herds have now got to walk to Egypt!

Solomon's fleet

King Solomon has just built a splendid fleet of ships.

Some of the new ships are based on the Red Sea on Israel's southern coast and trade with countries as far away as Arabia. They leave Israel with cargoes of copper and return, sometimes years later, with gold, peacocks, baboons, sandalwood and precious stones.

Other ships in the fleet sail the Mediterranean, trading with places like Egypt and Lebanon. Here at Joppa, the harbour is full of ships from all over the Mediterranean world.

Logs from the Lebanon

These are cedar logs for the new temple that King Solomon is building in Jerusalem. They've been provided by Hiram, King of Tyre, who lives further up the coast. Teams of men have chopped down trees, dragged them to the sea and floated the logs down to Joppa – a distance of about 150 kilometres.

Solomon's workmen

On Solomon's orders, 70,000 carriers are hard at work bringing wood and stone to Jerusalem for the temple. Here are just a few of them.

King Solomon's letter to King Hiram:

Dear King Hiram,
Please supply logs for my new temple. My men will work with yours, and I'll also pay your men's wages.
signed,
SOLOMON of ISRAEL
P.S. your men are the best in the world at cutting down trees.

King Hiram's reply:

Dear King Solomon,
Certainly. You can have all the logs you want. I'll have them cut down and floated by sea to any place you wish. In return you can give me food for my royal household.
signed
HIRAM of TYRE

Fair exchange

In return for the logs, Solomon is sending provisions back to King Hiram. Every year he gives him two thousand tons of wheat and four hundred thousand litres of olive oil.

Ships for peace and war

Ships built for trade are slow with high prows and sterns. Warships, on the other hand, are fast and streamlined. This one, from Phoenicia, has a pointed ram for sinking enemy boats.

Foreign imports

These horses and chariots have been imported from Egypt. Solomon will keep some of them and export the rest to kings in neighbouring countries.

Egyptian war chariots are the best in the world – and the most expensive. A good model costs about seven kilograms of gold.

Royal transport

Solomon himself is coming to watch the unloading. His litter is made of finest wood from the Lebanon, with silver posts and a gold base.

Phoenician ships

The best sailors in the ancient world were the Phoenicians. Their ships – called galleys – had oars and a sail. Sometimes the prow was shaped like a horse's head and the stern like a fish's tail. These ships sailed right across the Mediterranean and out into the Atlantic. Some of them even reached Britain. About six hundred years before Jesus, Phoenician ships sailed all the way round Africa.

When Solomon needed help to build his fleet, he naturally asked the Phoenicians. King Hiram provided him with shipbuilders and sailors, and most of Solomon's ships had Phoenician crews.

Journey into danger

Nehemiah, a Jew, is in exile far from home in the city of Susa. He was taken there when Jerusalem was captured by the Babylonians. Now he works in the palace serving wine for King Artaxerxes.

One day Nehemiah's brother arrives from Jerusalem. "Bad news," he says. "Jerusalem is in ruins. The walls are broken down and the gates have been burned."

Nehemiah wants to help, but what can he do? He asks God to guide him.

2

4 At last Nehemiah is on his way.

Ambush?
Could these be bandits? Nehemiah and his companions need to keep a constant look-out.

Rivers to cross
This is the River Tigris. Beyond is the River Euphrates. Nehemiah will need to cross them both.

Border patrol
It's a good thing Nehemiah asked the king for letters. Otherwise these soldiers might not have let him through.

Babylonian guard
Armed guards provided by the king to keep Nehemiah safe.

"Why are you looking so sad?" asks the king one day as Nehemiah is pouring his wine.

Nehemiah takes a deep breath. "Why shouldn't I look sad," he says, "when Jerusalem is in ruins?"

"What is it you want?" replies the king.

Nervously, Nehemiah asks permission to go back and rebuild Jerusalem. To his great surprise, the king agrees.

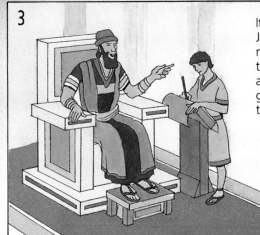

3

It's a long journey from Susa to Jerusalem – about 800 miles. Nehemiah needs to be sure that he can travel safely through the countries in between. He asks the king to write letters to the governors of those countries telling them to let him through.

"Of course I will," says the king.

Timber from the king's forests to help rebuild Jerusalem.

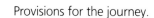

Provisions for the journey.

Difficult country

Nehemiah has just come over these mountains from Susa. Deserts and more mountains lie ahead of him before he reaches Jerusalem.

5

After weeks of travelling, Nehemiah reaches Jerusalem. After dark he sets about inspecting the damage.

6

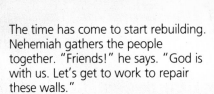

The time has come to start rebuilding. Nehemiah gathers the people together. "Friends!" he says. "God is with us. Let's get to work to repair these walls."

On the road with Paul and Luke

We have moved forward 500 years since the time of Nehemiah. It is now about fifteen years since Jesus died. Paul and his friend, Luke, have just arrived by ship in the country of Macedonia. (Now part of Greece, Macedonia was then a province in the Roman Empire.) The two travellers are here to tell people about Jesus, and they're hurrying to the city of Philippi, where Paul is hoping to stay. Behind them is the harbour and the ship they have just left; in front, the long, straight road to their destination.

Keep off the road!

In the Roman Empire, paved road are for soldiers and official government messengers only. Ordinary pedestrians like Paul and Luke must use the dirt track that runs alongside.

Essential kit for travellers: a stick, money-belt, and a hollowed-out gourd weighted with a stone for drawing water from wells.

Danger! Men at work

The Romans build their roads as straight as possible. They're made in three layers. The first is of stones mixed with cement to produce a kind of concrete. This is covered with gravel, rubble and broken pottery. The top layer is large stones, closely fitted together. The road slopes at the side so that water will drain off into the gutter.

'Food for 24, please'

Soldiers can claim free meals and lodging anywhere they like when they're on the march.

Queue here for taxis

Horse-drawn gigs are kept at posting stations along the main roads and can be hired like taxis. Drivers can be fined for careless driving. Some taxis even have a kind of meter – a cogwheel contraption that drops a pebble into a box for every mile travelled.

Beware pickpockets!

Inns are dangerous places, as this traveller is about to discover.

Along all the main routes, the government has built official inns. These are about a day's journey apart, with smaller hostels in between for slower travellers. A day's journey is reckoned to be sixteen to twenty miles.

ROME

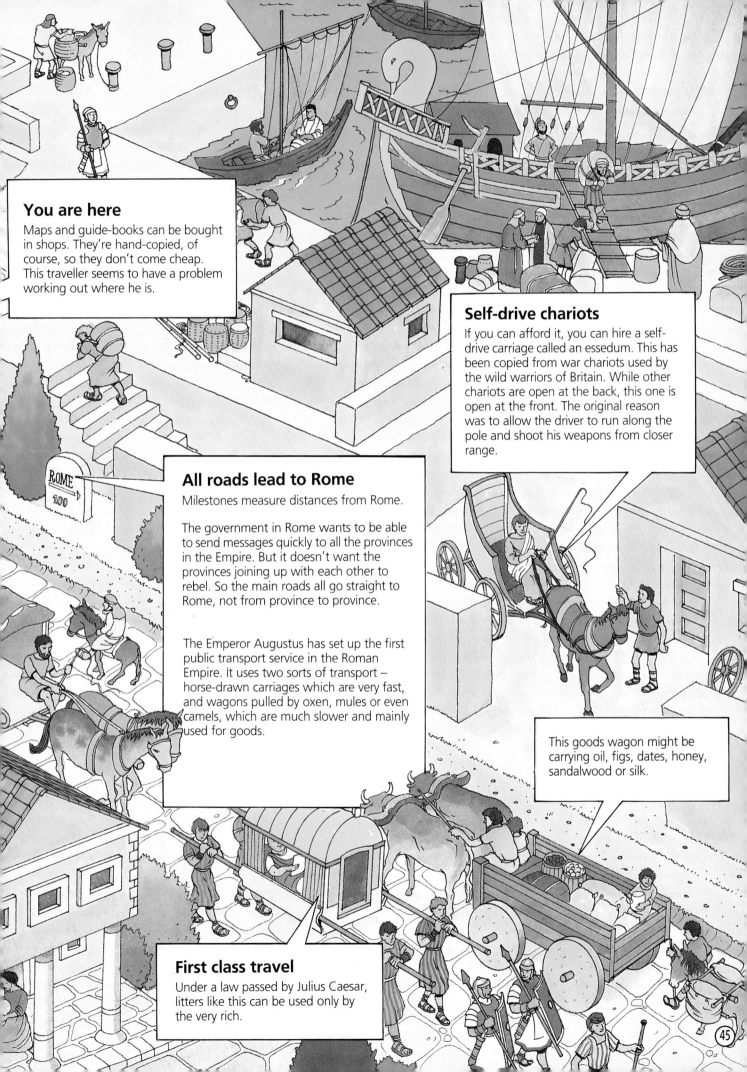

You are here

Maps and guide-books can be bought in shops. They're hand-copied, of course, so they don't come cheap. This traveller seems to have a problem working out where he is.

Self-drive chariots

If you can afford it, you can hire a self-drive carriage called an essedum. This has been copied from war chariots used by the wild warriors of Britain. While other chariots are open at the back, this one is open at the front. The original reason was to allow the driver to run along the pole and shoot his weapons from closer range.

All roads lead to Rome

Milestones measure distances from Rome.

The government in Rome wants to be able to send messages quickly to all the provinces in the Empire. But it doesn't want the provinces joining up with each other to rebel. So the main roads all go straight to Rome, not from province to province.

The Emperor Augustus has set up the first public transport service in the Roman Empire. It uses two sorts of transport – horse-drawn carriages which are very fast, and wagons pulled by oxen, mules or even camels, which are much slower and mainly used for goods.

This goods wagon might be carrying oil, figs, dates, honey, sandalwood or silk.

ROME
100

First class travel

Under a law passed by Julius Caesar, litters like this can be used only by the very rich.

45

How does your day compare?

In some ways life in Bible times was not very different from life today. In other ways it was completely different.

Here are some of the things we have seen people doing in this book. When you have found them, see if you can answer the questions. Afterwards you can check your answers over

FOOD

CLOTHES

GROWING UP

This girl is having a special meal with her family. Look at page 6 to find out what they were eating and drinking.

This is the kind of head covering Jesus would have worn as a boy. How is it made? See page 15.

This Egyptian schoolboy on page 26 throws away his work when the lesson is over. What is he writing on?

This girl is grinding grain. What did she make with it? See page 9.

This is Caleb at his uncle Nathan's wedding. What is he wearing? See page 12.

Zebedee, on page 28, is only ten but he is learning a trade. What is it?

Most of our food today is different.

Your clothes are probably quite different, unless you live in the Middle East.

Your books and pens are quite different and you will be much older before you leave school.

the page.

This will help you to see which things are like your life today and which are different. You can probably find many more things to compare as you look through the book.

LEISURE

These boys on page 32 are practising their skill at hitting a target. What are they using?

This game on page 30 is still played today. What is it?

Some of the games you play today have been around for a very long time. Others have changed.

RELIGION

What has this boy on page 34 come to the Temple to see?

Which musical instrument are they using in worship on page 35?

Today we do not have animal sacrifices as part of our worship but we do have musical instruments and we now have the Bible.

TRAVEL

How does Solomon travel when he visits the harbour on page 41?

What was a Roman self-drive chariot called? See page 45.

Your ways of travel are probably very different from Bible times.

Index

Answers (page 46/47)

1 Roast lamb with bitter
   herbs, bread without
   yeast, wine
2 Flour which she used to
   make bread
3 A square of cloth held in
   place with a circle of cord
4 A white tunic and cloak
5 Bits of broken pottery
6 Fishing
7 Stones with slings
8 Leapfrog
9 The sacrifice on the Day
   of Atonement
10 A tambourine
11 He is carried in a litter
12 An essedum